Sea of Change: Flying the Outer Banks

Book, Text, and Photographs Copyright © 2015 Garrett Fisher. All rights reserved.

Maps Copyright © OpenStreetMap contributors. Map data, including map modifications made by the author, is available under the Open Database License, cartography licensed as CC-BY-SA. Please see openstreetmap.org, opendatacommons.org, and creativecommons.org.

ISBN: 069240869X
ISBN-13: 978-0692408698

Published by Tenmile Publishing LLC - Alpine, WY
Website & Blog: garrettfisher.me

All photos in this book are available as prints, digital files, and framed prints. Please visit the website.

Front Cover: Cape Lookout **Above:** Hatteras Inlet, Ocracoke Island

ABOVE: *Northern OBX Photograph Locations (page number).* **BELOW:** *Southern OBX Photograph Locations.*

ABOVE: *Atlantic Ocean & Shackleford Banks.*

BELOW: *Shackleford Banks & Back Sound.*

LEFT: *Shackleford Banks.* **ABOVE & BELOW:** *Back Sound Marshes.*

ABOVE & BELOW: *Core Sound Marsh & Cape Lookout National Seashore.* **RIGHT:** *Back Sound Marsh.*

LEFT: *Lookout Bight & Cape Lookout Lighthouse.* **ABOVE & BELOW:** *Cape Lookout Lighthouse.*

Photographing Constant Motion

When I set out to complete a book project, I start with a personal mission. In just about every case, I am trying to capture the essence of something, and generally something that is difficult, counterintuitive, or fleeting. In the case of the Outer Banks, I had little in the way of expectation, and found that the Outer Banks themselves called the shots on what I was doing, instead of the other way around.

My prior projects have had a sufficient portion of the subject grounded in the finite, meaning that there was something tangible I could base my work on. In my flagship book about the 58 peaks over 14,000 feet in Colorado, it was a matter of wrestling the plane and atmosphere into submission so I could capture epic spires of rock. In the case of the Outer Banks, it would be tempting to fall into the trap

Above:

Back Sound, with Shackleford Banks in the distance. Atlantic Ocean on the horizon.

Right:

Marshlands in Back Sound, not far from Rachel Carson Preserve.

of merely *documenting* them, when doing just that misses their personality entirely.

The essence of the Outer Banks is change. I think I can speak for those who love living or visiting there by stating that we love the OBX for that very reason. Sand, surf, and sky are in a constantly rhythmic state of change, and it bespeaks tremendous wonder that we can spend time on effectively mobile islands, sticking out into a changing sea, at the convergence of two major Atlantic Ocean currents.

The thing about visiting a new place is that it enthralls just about any visitor for a temporary period. While I had been to the OBX many times, I had only flown through once, just enough to know it is pretty. Just one visit in the air is only enough to capture the initial mo-

ment of discovery, and it is a human tendency to document the experience more so than the essence of the place. How can a place be properly understood if the photographer has laid eyes on it only once? Thus, I knew that I would be photographing the OBX, I just didn't know what my focus would be. For the first time in my writing career, I decided to let the subject talk to me.

Talk to me it did. Every single time I flew, the sand, ocean, currents, inlets, and sky looked different. It was not just a matter of minor differences, it was a matter of wholesale surprises each time I revisited certain places. The more I saw, the more I realized that the bulk of the surface area of the water near the Outer Banks is undiscovered. Visitors are relegated to NC 12 and assorted side streets, while I flew above them in complete freedom, able to see sound, sand, and ocean all in one. There is an entire world of marshes, currents, and sand patterns that make the Outer Banks many times more beautiful than most of us realize. It didn't take too long to figure out that the most profound contribution I could have would be to bring the Outer Banks that people do not know to them, showing these unknown and poorly accessed areas in ways that are difficult if not impossible to see on the ground.

ABOVE:

Tip of Cape Lookout (left) looking out over unstable sand patterns jutting into the Atlantic.

LEFT:

Marshes of Back Sound, behind Cape Lookout National Seashore.

Even more so, there is so much of the Outer Banks that lies beneath the surface of the water that becomes visible when getting high above it. When looking out over the water from the beach or a boat, the field of view is much smaller than rising high above it. Flying around these beautiful waters let me peer into the soul of the Outer Banks, and what I found was a stunning collection of colors, waves, patterns, and swirls, leaving me in sheer awe every time I look at it again.

Above: *Cape Lookout.*   **Below:** *Lookout Bight.*   **Right:** *Cape Lookout Lighthouse.*

LEFT: *Cape Lookout National Seashore.*   **BELOW:** *Lots of Dolpins.*   **ABOVE:** *Lots of Birds.*

LEFT: *Five Ocean Currents, Cape Lookout National Seashore.* **ABOVE:** *Ophelia Inlet.*

ALL: *Ophelia Inlet, Cape Lookout National Seashore.*

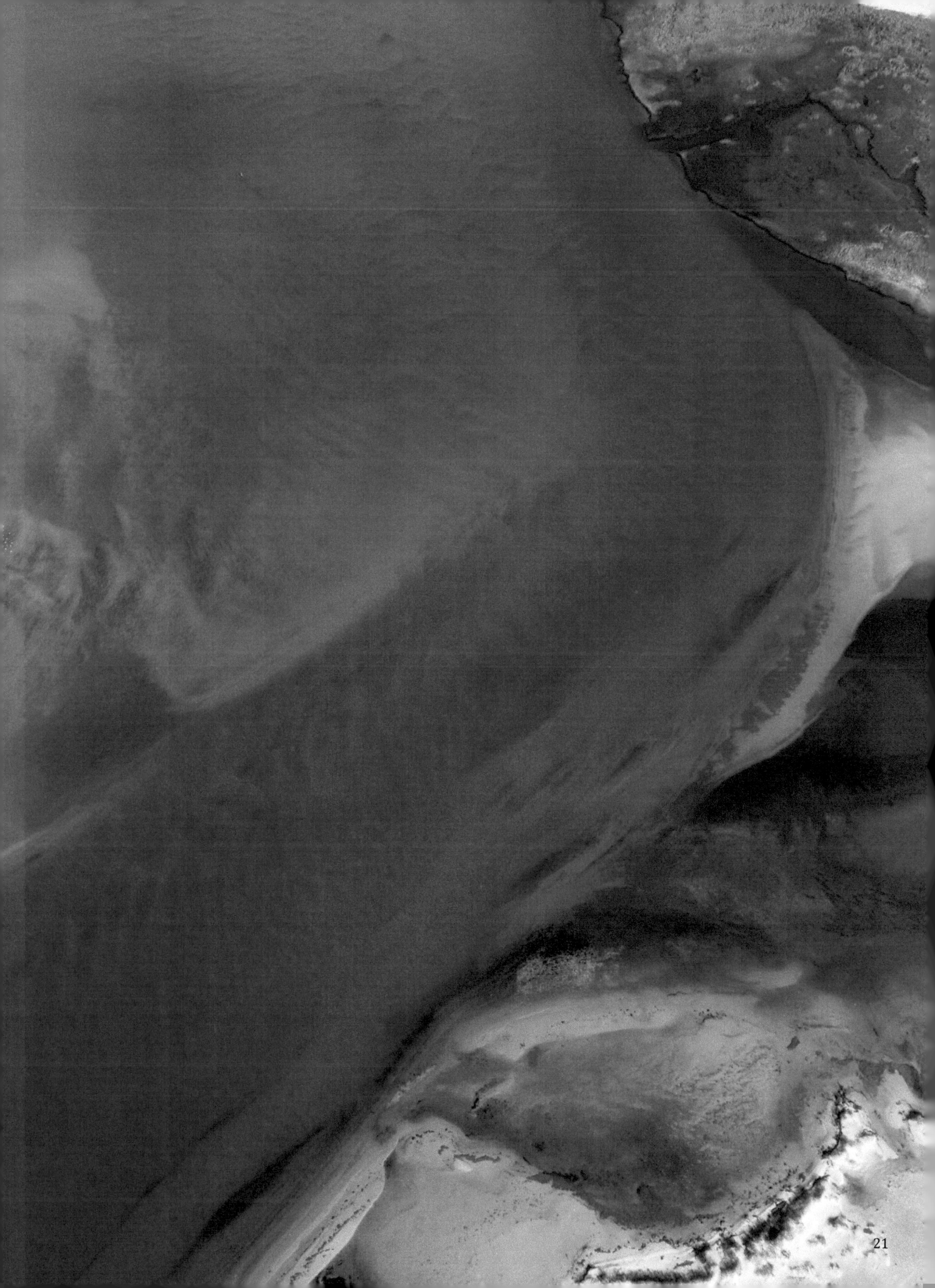

ALL: *Ophelia Inlet, Cape Lookout National Seashore.*

ABOVE & RIGHT: *Ophelia Inlet, Cape Lookout National Seashore.* **BELOW:** *Core Sound, east of Ophelia Inlet.*

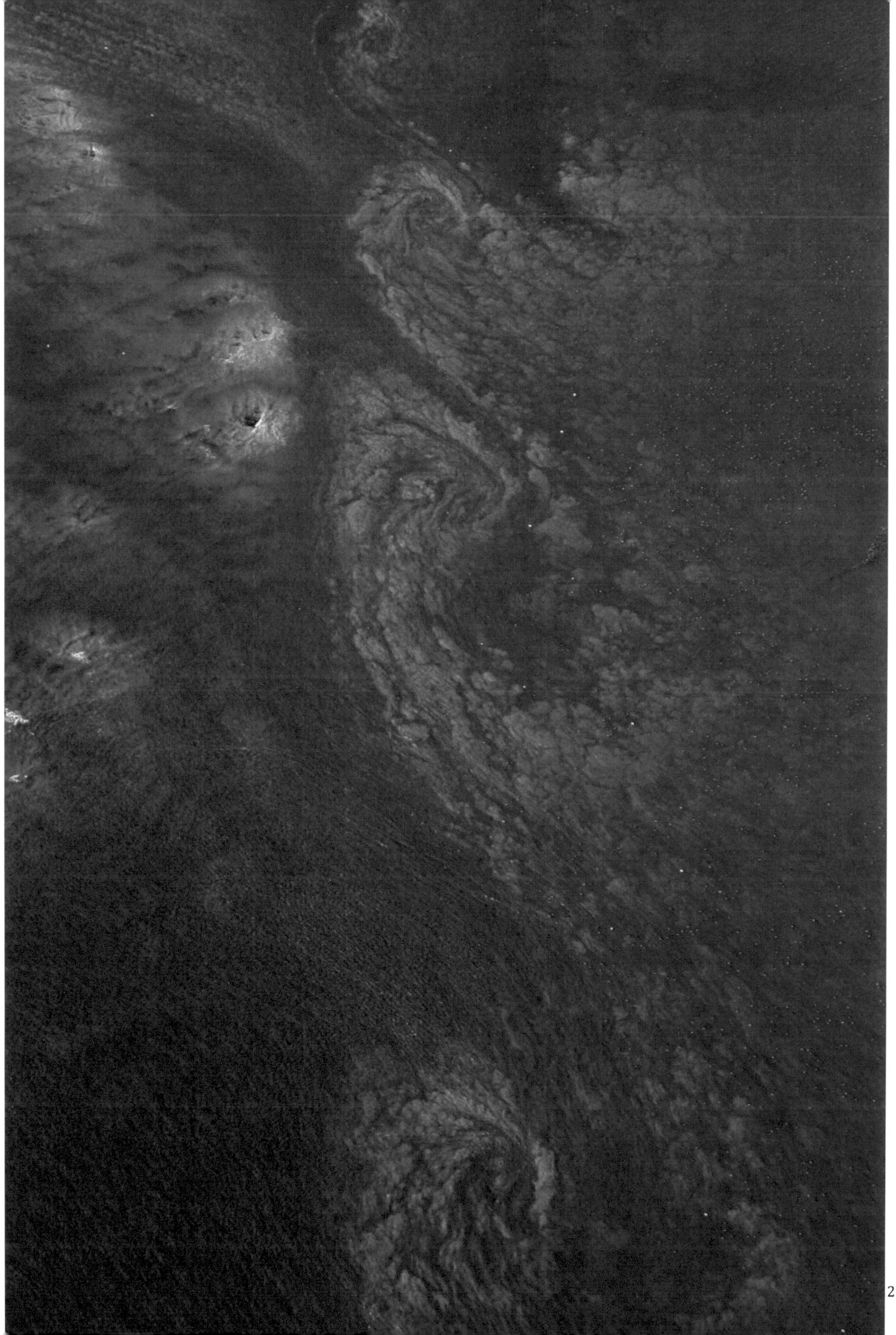

ALL: *Ophelia Inlet, Cape Lookout National Seashore.*

ALL: *Ophelia Inlet, Cape Lookout National Seashore.*

ALL: *New Drum Inlet, Cape Lookout National Seashore.*

BELOW: *New Drum Inlet.* **ABOVE & RIGHT:** *Convergence of Atlantic Ocean currents.*

LEFT: *Portsmouth Island, Cape Lookout National Seashore.*   **ABOVE:** *Sound side marsh, Portsmouth Island.*

LEFT: *Ocean Currents, Cape Lookout National Seashore.*   ABOVE: *Sound side marsh, Portsmouth Island.*

Flying the Outer Banks

My introduction to the Outer Banks from the air took place in late 2011. A friend of mine was getting married soon, and we decided to use the impending restrictions of wedlock as an excuse to do something fun beforehand. Flying from Charlotte, NC, we followed highways to US 64, all the way to Dare County Regional Airport in Manteo. At the time, I did not possess a GPS, so I navigated entirely by dead reckoning and pilotage. Translation: I read a map and looked out the window. The aircraft has no radio, and the only onboard navigation "instrument" is a compass.

As we arrived at Manteo, my compatriot had a bad case of nausea. He had vomited once prior when I was flying, so this was no surprise. We drove into town in the loaner car, acquired Dramamine, and after taking it, he promptly vomited on the side of the road, passersby looking at us like we were town drunks.

With that out of the way, we were back in the air, cruising from Manteo down toward Hatteras, our intended camping destination. I was in sheer glee. It was unbelievably beautiful, water on both sides, and I was photographing left and right, while unknown to me, my passenger was vomiting, again. Finally, he yelled from the backseat "STOP TAKING PICTURES!" Now my fun was ruined, so I deposited him at the airport, much to his satisfaction, and took some flights around Hatteras island.

ABOVE & RIGHT:

Marshes on the Pamlico Sound side of Portsmouth Island, Cape Lookout National Seashore.

The next day, we flew down Ocracoke and over Cape Lookout National Seashore, my photography restricted to straight and level flight, fueling at Morehead City, and went home. The whole affair was interesting, and enough to tell me that I certainly wanted more.

As we came out for the winter, I quickly learned that I can't just fly a section of the Outer Banks and declare that I captured it. Photographing the scenery here is like trying to catch wind, one is attempting to finalize in permanence a fleeting subject. It did not take long to realize that I needed to fly the length of the island chain many times, in many circumstances, to convey the magnitude of what I was looking at.

Tactically speaking, I was unprepared for the weather at the coast. It is far more humid than Charlotte, and just because a cold front comes through, it does not mean the air gets clear. Water is effectively on three sides, sometimes four, so it is safe to state that the air is quite humid, most of the time. Humidity creates a haze. Haze creates glare, and glare is amplified by reflecting off of water. It was a regular chase trying to get conditions where the lighting was ideal, and after months of flying and fixating on the matter, I was able to get some resplendent days with dry air sourced out of the Southwestern US, a very small minority of the weather. It did not help that the winter was the coldest since most people reading this book have been born.

ABOVE:

Ocracoke, NC and Ocracoke Island.

LEFT:

Ocean currents, Ocracoke Inlet with Portsmouth Island in distance, on a stormy day.

Oddly, I had a fear of flying over water that I needed to overcome. For some reason, I really, really do not like flying over water, and I am not sure why. The year prior to this book, I completed photographing all 58 peaks over 14,000 feet from the same airplane, mostly in winter. That did not scare me like water does. Furthermore, in 1999, I rented a Cessna in Buffalo NY and flew it to Toronto Canada, in November, crossing Lake Ontario. This event was soon after the JFK Jr. tragedy, a result of losing reference to the horizon and crashing into the Atlantic. As we left the shore of the Niagara Peninsula, visibility was poor, and we could not see land anywhere for quite

Above:

Village of Ocracoke, NC.

Right:

Tip of southern end of Ocracoke Island, jutting out into the Pamlico Sound. Portsmouth Island in background.

awhile before reaching Toronto. Winds were strong, and Lake Ontario was 43 degrees Fahrenheit, affording about 15 minutes of useful body temperature if the airplane engine quit. That did not bother me. Flying over water in all directions on the coast did. Eventually, I was able to conquer it by doing enough of it to be rational about the situation. Ninety-nine percent of the time, I was over land on the Outer Banks, or in gliding range to it. A fraction of the time I ventured out in the Atlantic to view tidal currents spilling out of inlets, and it would have been a stretch to say that I could have made land if I needed to glide in.

al fog can do some weird things, and I did fly around it twice, though the situation is avoidable if one wishes to err on the side of caution; I was trying to capture the fog. Salt is a risk to the airframe from a maintenance perspective, and I found myself rinsing the airplane off after flying long runs along the coast. Wind is strong, though Dare County Airport has two runways, reducing the crosswind factor extensively. All in all, it was a pleasant experience, with many surprises and challenges. I must say that I am extremely surprised with the beauty I saw, even after having flown out here many years ago.

The technical nature of flying the coast is not too terribly complex. There are some military airspaces which make things tight, requiring vigilance in certain areas. I learned early on that shorebirds are not to be messed with, and should be carefully avoided at all costs. Coast-

I found that it was tempting to spend time photographing the popular, inhabited places of the OBX, though I found that those were the least compelling photographs. The best things to chase were completely unpredictable: ocean currents, tidal flows, ocean colors, and inlet ac-

tivity. While there is a correlation to wind and rough seas, that did little to tell me the water sources at the inlets. "Water sources?" you might say. Indeed, the water going to and from the sounds to the ocean sourced in different areas. The Albemarle, Croatan, and Currituck Sounds have more fresh water, and also more water sourced from rivers that traverse swampy areas. Those swampy rivers are completely opaque, with dark brown color, and can be drawn into the inlets and oceans. A storm may pile water up into the Pamlico Sound, and on the clear days after, the water rushes out, carrying dirty river water with it. Another storm may push water out of the Pamlico Sound, resulting in clear Gulf Stream water rushing in after the storm, making the inlets shine like the Caribbean. I gave up assuming what it would do, and simply photographed it extensively.

ABOVE:

Pamlico Sound and Ocracoke Island, looking northeast, from the NE side of Ocracoke village.

LEFT:

Sand patterns under the water, Ocracoke Inlet.

PAGE 46:

Southern tip of Ocracoke Island.

PAGE 47:

Pamlico Sound & Ocracoke Island.

Many wonder what it is like to photograph while flying. I go into some extensive detail on the subject in a separate book, "Appalachian Altitude: Flying the Highest Peaks of the South." When it comes to the OBX, I thankfully did not have anything to worry about flying into, such as large mountains. There also were not downdrafts coming off of mountains, threatening to swat me out of the sky. In that respect, it was relaxing and pleasant not to have to worry about those factors. Generally, I found myself traversing the islands at 45 degree angles, so I could get a shot looking down the island without aircraft parts in it. My biggest concern was birds and other airplanes, as the thin islands create a focal point for other air traffic. Otherwise, flying in the OBX is a lot like cruising the beach: enjoyable, pleasant, and relaxed.

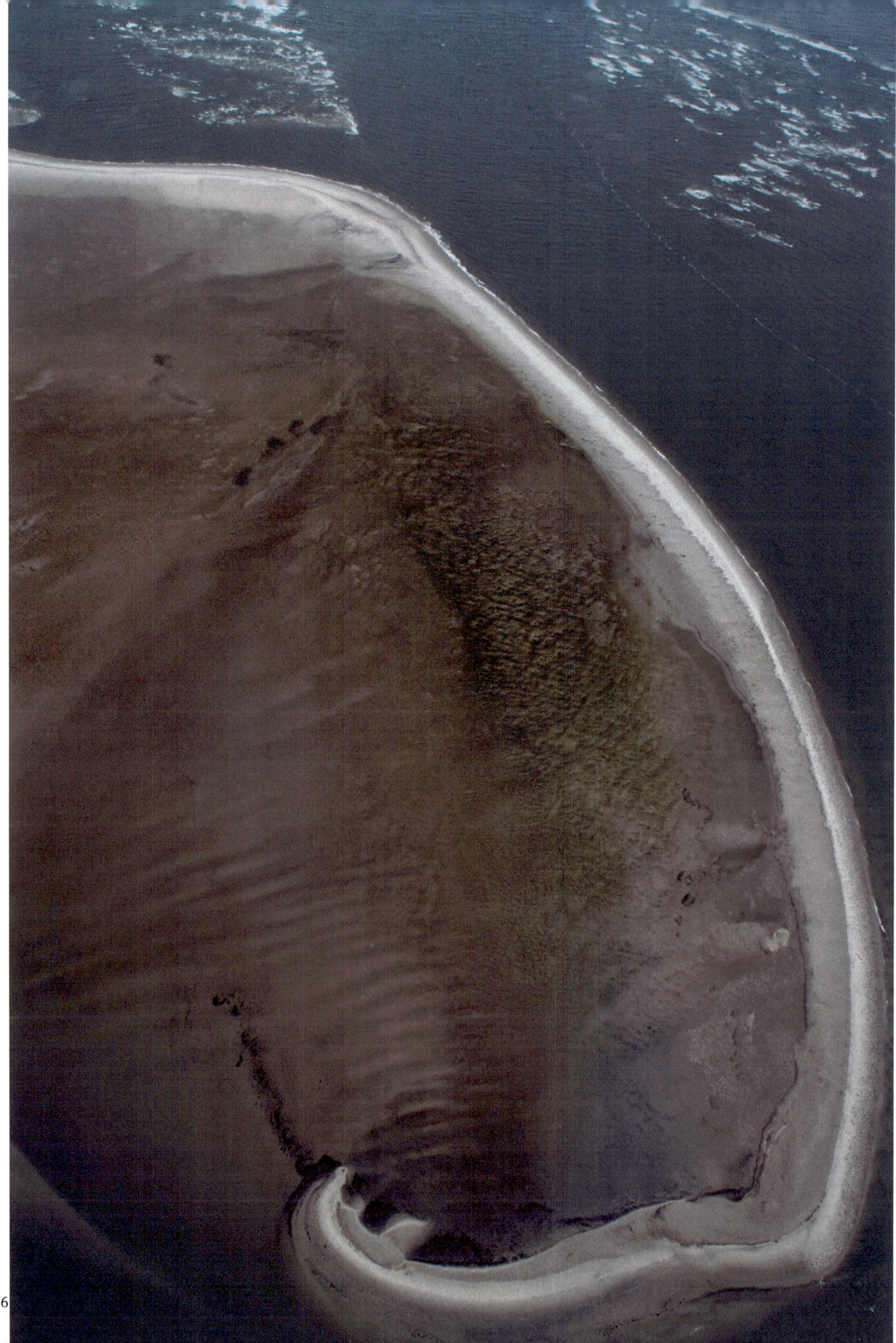

LEFT: *Ocracoke Island & marshes.* **ABOVE:** *Sound side marsh, Ocracoke Island.*

LEFT & BELOW: *Hatteras Inlet, Ocracoke to the left.*   **ABOVE:** *Hatteras Inlet, Ocracoke Island.*

ABOVE: *Hatteras Inlet, Hatteras Island.* **BELOW:** *Cape Hatteras* **RIGHT:** *Western tip of Hatteras Island.*

THE SEA OF CHANGE

It is evident even from the ground how mobile life on the barrier islands of the Outer Banks is. Fragile spits of sand protrude grand distances into the ocean, a product of ocean currents, weather, and river systems, creating a fragile balance that peaks its head above land. Very little about what we see is permanent, as the islands are on the move, both naturally, and as a result of sea level changes. While political forces affecting the Outer Banks have declared that climate change is irrelevant, the islands are still moving, whether people like it or not.

It is very evident how interconnected the presence of the islands is to the sand and ocean patterns under the water. Many photos in this book show that an oversized sand dune that may comprise an island is also an underwater ridge, where water is shallower, and one can see an extension of the land underneath. Other images show the ocean scouring into an existing landmass, and depositing the sand elsewhere.

Differing ocean and sound currents would collide in one place, visible from the air by virtue of different colors, and the sand underneath moved as a result, being found in a different place next time I flew over. This back and forth, push and pull existence has been going on for a very long time, and is going to continue into the future, a continuous painting being repainted on an ongoing basis, curiously remaining stunning no matter what we end up seeing.

The only "problem" with such mobility is our Western approach to land ownership and housing. Property lines are fixed in stone, and when the island vanishes underneath a million dollar house and a real property line,

LEFT:

Hatteras Bight.

ABOVE:

Cape Hatteras, looking east.

the effect is highly disruptive, only because we choose to have it that way. The same approach to housing and property that we use in rolling farmland of the Midwest is the same approach we use to mobile sand. Clearly, that will cause more and more problems into the future, as billions of dollars of real estate sit on the edge of predictable destruction.

It is not that I am saying that living on the OBX is a bad thing. It is readily evident from the air how we as a society have chosen to build an extremely expensive and fragile infrastructure, and we seem to whine as though it is a disaster when there are losses. Houses could be seen from the air, literally tipping into the sea, and the building craze continues unabated, a sizable waste of money. Perhaps some of the individuals that choose to build ought

Above:

NC 12, north of Avon, with Pamlico Sound and marshes in the background.

Right:

NC 12 just north of Buxton, as the highway leaves the main section of Hatteras Island.

Pages 58-59:

NC 12 on Hatteras Island.

to consider a plane ride over their proposed parcel of mobile sand beforehand.

The many times I have visited the OBX in advance of our winter there, I knew that things changed, though I was not there enough or long enough to fathom what the changes were, exactly. The more I flew, the more I saw just how much everything I could see from the air was changing, and the more I wanted to go up and see what nature had put on display this particular week. If you are fortunate to visit the OBX more than once, I suggest keeping a keen eye to how different things are one visit to the next. If you like a particular scene, enjoy it before it changes!

ABOVE: *Travails of building on the ocean.* **BELOW:** *Oregon Inlet sand patterns.* **RIGHT:** *Oregon Inlet Bridge.*

LEFT: *Pier, Rodanthe NC.*   **BELOW:** *Oregon Inlet, Pamlico & Roanoke Sound currents.*   **ABOVE:** *Oregon Inlet.*

BOTH: *Oregon Inlet on different days, showing different currents and colors.*

LEFT: *Bodie Island Lighthouse.* **ABOVE:** *US 64 Bridge over Croatan Sound in fog.* **BELOW:** *Nags Head Pier.*

ABOVE: *Marsh south of Wanchese.*　　**BELOW:** *Jockeys Ridge.*　　**RIGHT:** *US 64 Bridge over Roanoke Sound.*

LEFT: *Row Houses, Duck & Corolla line.* **ABOVE & BELOW:** *Currituck Sound, Corolla.*

ABOVE: *Whalehead Club & Currituck Lighthouse.*   **BELOW:** *Corolla 4x4 access ramp.*   **RIGHT:** *4x4 Beach, Corolla.*

Left: *Penny Hill, 4x4 Beach.* **Above:** *Horse, 4x4 Beach, Corolla.* **Below:** *Ocean Current, 4x4 Beach.*

BOTH: *Corolla 4x4 Beach, showing no paved roads anywhere.*

BOTH: *False Cape State Park, Virginia, the northern terminus of the Outer Banks.*

More Books by the Author

Photo Credit: Adam Romer

With a thirst for new and interesting perspectives, Garrett Fisher is perpetually adventure flying, undertaking a variety of projects at any given moment. Currently, he lives on an airpark in Wyoming outside of Yellowstone, where he is working on a host of book projects, two of which will focus on Grand Teton National Park and Yellowstone National Park. He blogs about the flights he takes to explore and document things from the air, providing an abundance of photographs and maps on his website at www.garrettfisher.me.